Lucy Sings
on Lucy Street

Written by **LAWRENCE ROBERTS** and **SALLY-ANN ROBERTS**
Illustrated by **JESTENIA SOUTHERLAND**
Epilogue by **ROBIN ROBERTS**

HARPER
An Imprint of HarperCollinsPublishers

There was once a little girl named Lucy, who lived on Lucy Street. Eight-year-old Lucimarian Tolliver was called Lucy by her playmates, who also lived there. Lucy Street was a tree-lined road dotted with simple two-story homes in Akron, Ohio. Young Lucy lived in the middle of the block, and her grandparents lived at the end.

The little girl with caramel-colored skin and thick, fluffy hair was a rare sight to many of the European immigrants in the neighborhood. One child innocently asked if Lucy and her best friend, Wanda, could wash off their color.

Lucy laughed and asked, "Can you wash off your freckles?"

On one sunny summer morning in 1932, Lucy was playing hide-and-seek with her best friend, Wanda, and the other children in the neighborhood. They all had something in common: poverty. People around the country were losing their jobs. Lots of people were having a hard time paying for food and keeping their homes. Playing hide-and-seek gave the children a break from the problems at home.

"Gotcha, Lucia!" Mario shouted as he pulled Lucy from the bushes.

It was Lucy's turn to be the seeker. As she began counting, the kids scattered like ants. ". . . Ninety-seven, ninety-eight, ninety-nine, one hundred! Ready or not, here I come!"

Then she whirled around, ready for the chase. But suddenly Lucy stopped. Her smile disappeared. Lucy's eyes widened with panic.

Wanda peeked out from her hiding place when she heard her best friend scream.
She caught up with Lucy as Lucy began running wildly toward her house.
"Lucy, what's wrong?" Wanda wailed.

Lucy pointed down the street. Then Wanda saw the men walking out of Lucy's house carrying a sofa. Together, the friends ran toward the men as they shoved the sofa into the back of a truck.

The girls burst inside.
"Mama, what's going on?" Lucy asked, panting to catch her breath. Her eyes bulged as the men walked back in.

Wearily, Mama embraced her daughter and explained. "Lucimarian, we can't keep paying for the furniture, so we have to give it back to the store."

Wanda gently patted Lucy's back.

Moved by the little girl's compassion, Mama touched the child's head. "Wanda, you are a good friend." Then Mama stooped down to look into Lucy's eyes. "Everything is going to be all right. Don't worry your little head none."

The men picked up the dining table next. "Mama, where are we gonna eat?" Lucy looked in horror at the empty living room. "Where are we gonna read?"

"Child, we are going to do what we always do. Trust the Lord." Mama placed her arms around Lucy's and Wanda's shoulders and walked them to the door. "Now it's time to get to getting. These men have work to do. Go outside and play."

The two little girls left, quietly sidestepping the men who went to collect more of the Tollivers' furniture.

Once outside, Wanda broke the silence. "Lucy, it's going to be okay."

"No, it's not!" Lucy said, bursting into tears.

Then Wanda had an idea. She walked Lucy down the street to a place where Wanda knew her friend could find help.

Pastor George was sitting on his front porch.

"Grandpa!" Lucy cried. She left Wanda on the sidewalk and bounded up the steps and into her grandfather's arms. Grandpa George smiled and waved at Wanda as she nodded in return and began to head home.

"Grandpa, some men are taking all our furniture!" Lucy explained between sobs.

"Shh, shh, child," Grandpa George murmured as he patted Lucy's quivering arm. "The whole country is sufferin' right now. A lot of folks like your daddy and mama are having trouble finding work and paying bills. It's bad now, but trust me, it's gonna get better."

"When is it gonna get better?" Lucy demanded.
"And what are we gonna do till then?"
Grandpa George let out a deep breath.

Then he smiled and leaned back on the porch swing. "It's like that song you learned in Sunday school," he told Lucy.

He started swinging back and forth with Lucy in his arms and began to sing.

"This little light of mine,
I'm gonna let it shine.
This little light of mine . . ."

"Sing with me, Lucy," said Grandpa George.
"I don't feel like singing." Lucy pouted.

Grandpa George stopped swinging and gently turned her face upward to gaze intently into her eyes.

"Singing is good medicine, child. It cures all kinds of ills. When you sing, you cheer yourself up. There's a mean old goblin who wants us to feel sad. He wants us to think there is no hope. But that goblin can't stick around for long when we sing a happy song. Let's give it a try."

Grandpa George started to stomp his feet to the rhythm.

"This little light of mine, I'm gonna let it shine. This little light of mine, I'm gonna let it shine. This little light of mine, I'm gonna let it shine. Let it shine. Let it shine. Let it shine."

Lucy joined in, reluctantly at first. But she was singing strongly by the time they reached the second verse. She sang loud enough for her friends to hear, and they joined in on the sidewalk.

"Everywhere I go, I'm gonna let it shine. Everywhere I go, I'm gonna let it shine.
Everywhere I go, I'm gonna let it shine. Let it shine! Let it shine! Let it shine!"

Lucy giggled as Grandpa smiled. Then he said, "Lookee
here, a few minutes ago, you were all teared up and sad.
How ya feeling now, Lucy?"

She jumped up, and her smile disappeared. She saw the men getting into the cab of the truck. "Those men are taking our furniture, and I don't know what we're gonna do." Lucy frowned. "Singing feels good, but it doesn't change anything."

Grandpa George looked at Lucy and said, "But *you* will."

"What do you mean?" Lucy asked.

"You are going to do great and wonderful things in your life."

"Really? How do you know?" Lucy asked.

"You have a gift, Lucimarian. When you sing, you make people feel better. Your grandmother Lizzie and I pray every day for you and your sister and brother to be held in the favor of the people."

"What does that mean—favor of the people?" Lucy asked.

"That means we are asking the Lord to bring people across your path who will help you. They're like earth angels."

"Like you, Grandpa? You're my earth angel."

He gave his granddaughter a big hug and said, "Just do one thing for me, Lucimarian."

"What?"

"Life is filled with ups and downs. No matter what, keep a song in your heart. Keep singing."

Lucy thought about it for a moment and then replied, "I will."

Grandpa George picked Lucy up for another hug, then set her down.
"You see, Wanda is waiting for you."
Lucy could see her best friend standing in the distance, waving. Lucy
skipped down the street to join Wanda.

"Are you okay? What did your grandpa say?"

"Grandpa said I should sing more. I don't know if I can be cheerful like Grandpa, but I guess I'm gonna try."

Wanda was quiet for a moment, then said, "I bet I can beat you to the end of the block!"

Lucy squinted at her best friend and said, "You're on! Ready! Set! Go!" And they were off.

That night, Lucy and her family sat in the basement at a table lit only by candles. The electricity had been turned off because the Tollivers could no longer pay their light bill. Lucy looked around at her downtrodden parents, William and Sally Tolliver, and her eleven-year-old big brother, William, who her parents lovingly called William Son. Her three-year-old baby sister, Dee, was fidgeting in her chair next to Mama.

Gloom settled on the dark basement like a fog. Upstairs, lawn furniture filled the once-comfortable living room. Yet they still had their beds to sleep in, and they had each other. Suddenly Lucy remembered what she had promised Grandpa George. She looked up from her plate of beans and smiled bravely. "I have a little song in my heart, and I want to sing it," she said.

Daddy wearily plopped his head into his hands. "No singing at the table. Eat your supper, Lucimarian," he said.

She finished her dinner quickly, then asked to be excused. Her father nodded, and she rushed up the stairs and out into the backyard.

Lucy knelt by the basement window and looked down onto the family she loved.
As loudly as she could, she sang,

"This little light of mine, I'm gonna let it shine!
This little light of mine, I'm gonna let it shine!
This little light of mine, I'm gonna let it shine!
Let it shine! Let it shine! Let it shine!"

Lucy's voice filled the dark night on Lucy Street with light. Lucy sang,

"Everywhere I go, I'm gonna let it shine.
Everywhere I go, I'm gonna let it shine!
Everywhere I go, I'm gonna let it shine.
Let it shine! Let it shine! Let it shine!"

The little girl with the big voice had no idea that her song was touching hearts throughout her neighborhood . . . just as it was in her family's basement.

Dee squealed with delight. William Son laughed. Mama smiled and so did Daddy as tears filled his eyes.

Lucy whirled around the backyard with satisfaction. Mission accomplished!

Epilogue

By ROBIN ROBERTS

"Okay, children, time to get to getting."

Eighteen-year-old Lucy silenced the boisterous Sunday school class. She sat at the piano, preparing to lead the kids in a song before the lesson. The Robert Street Church of God had been founded in Akron in 1917 by Lucy's grandfather, Rev. George Suddeth.

The small sanctuary was heated with a wood-burning stove during the bitter cold winter months. In the summer, churchgoers fanned themselves with cardboard fans provided by a local mortuary.

But on this spring day, May 31, 1942, they didn't need fans. A refreshing breeze blew through the church's open windows as the children settled in for Sunday school, which always preceded Rev. Suddeth's sermon.

Lucy played the piano and led the children in singing "This little light of mine, I'm gonna let it shine. This little light of mine, I'm gonna . . ."

"Lucimarian Tolliver, stand up!" The Sunday school superintendent abruptly interrupted the song. Lucy stood, not knowing that her life was about to change. Mr. Robinson could barely contain his joy as he walked over, clutching a newspaper. "Lucimarian," he said, placing his hand on her shoulder, "you are in the *Akron Beacon Journal*! Take a look!"

Lucy opened her eyes wide in disbelief when she saw her picture in the newspaper. Mr. Robinson held it up for all the children to see and announced proudly, "Lucy has won herself a John S. Knight scholarship! Young lady, you're going to college!"

Lucy gasped as the class erupted in applause and cheers. She only wished Wilma Schnegg could be there too. Miss Schnegg was one of the earth angels her grandfather George had predicted would cross her path so long ago. Wilma Schnegg was Lucy's enrichment teacher at Robinson Grammar School. She had planted the seed of college in Lucy's heart.

From the time Lucy was in the second grade through high school, Wilma Schnegg was there, laying out the road map for Lucy to get to college. And it worked! From taking the tough college prep courses to becoming a member of the National Honor Society and applying for the Knight scholarship. Wilma Schnegg had been an answer to her grandparents' prayers.

Grandpa George, who had been watching proudly from the back of the sanctuary, stepped forward. "Lucy, you are on your way. But always remember—"

Lucy ran into his arms. "I know, Grandpa. Always keep a song in my heart. I will always keep singing."

Singing was a gift that Lucy would share the rest of her life.